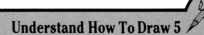

Understand How To Draw 5
Drawing Buildings and Towns
Clifford Bayly

SEARCH PRESS
Wellwood North Farm Road Tunbridge Wells

Introduction

Drawing buildings and towns is, generally speaking, more exacting than other forms of outdoor drawing. However, providing you can appreciate the necessity of working in a more deliberate and systematic manner in the early stages you should not find the subject-matter unduly difficult.

Buildings, most of which have hard clean lines, can be daunting for the beginner who finds drawing freehand straight lines difficult. But few buildings in fact contain absolutely straight lines as drawn with a ruler, for weather, age and damage all take toll on their fabric. Again, the lines of most buildings are broken by protuberances; while plants, trees, lampposts and other street furniture interrupt and soften them.

When you are drawing buildings, remember to keep a light touch to your work from the beginning and to use a searching, broken line. Too much attention to detail sometimes leads to a tight, rather too mechanical look to the finished work.

Try to spend most of your time working on location. Get used to the bustle of the roads and streets, and to making quick notes from a convenient viewpoint. Never mind the curious onlooker; you can always put him in your picture when he walks away!

Materials and equipment

If you are working at home, the usual range of pencils, pens, crayons, papers and sketchpads which you normally use are all suitable. However, when you venture outdoors to sketch, you will need to give your equipment some careful thought.

Whenever you can, reconnoitre the area around your chosen subject a day or two beforehand to see how convenient or inconvenient the viewpoints may be; for this will determine what kind of equipment you will be able to use. It is no use taking along a large layout pad to a busy street corner, or pots of ink where you can only sketch standing up. I always keep a basic kit which accompanies me in the car and when I am on foot.

I recommend a range of four or five graphite pencils; H for the fine linear work, and softer grades up to 6B for tones and shadows. A black carbon pencil, 2B grade, is excellent for general purpose sketching, especially on grained paper.

One of the most useful pencils is the watercolour pencil. It not only gives a good dense black on most papers; it has also the unique advantage of water-solubility — tones can be dissolved with a wet brush or even with a moistened finger, to give a line and wash effect. On the other hand, I do not recommend ballpoints as they tend to yield a monotonous line.

Fountain pens with a flexible nib are excellent if you prefer to work with pens, but never use Indian ink in one as it will clog. Also, be sure to refill your pen after using it — it is exasperating to run dry in the middle of a sketch!

I carry two sketchpads about with me: a small one that fits easily into my jacket pocket, and a larger one for the car. Both are ringbound, and of thickish paper because thin paper cockles whenever I wet it to use the watercolour pencil. Two grades of paper are sufficient: a fairly smooth cartridge and a rougher watercolour paper.

Siting and position

One of the most important aspects of drawing buildings is lighting. The shadows which buildings cast across the streets and across each other, architectural detail, and decoration all add the visual richness of the light and shade on a building. Sometimes, if the light is not right, a simple calculation will tell you when the sun will move so that your subject will be better lit. Cloudy days offer a chance to study line, mass and texture; and rainy days an opportunity (if you can sit in a café window) of studying reflections in wet streets and puddles.

Sometimes the most interesting and unusual viewpoints are not accessible from street level or are to be found inside private or industrial property. In such instances, it is worth writing to or calling on the clerk of works, foreman (or station master of a railway station) to get written permission which you can show to anyone who challenges your right to be there. Again, views from office windows high up above the rooftops offer wonderful scope — it is surprising how lucky one can be in obtaining permission to draw from unusual or what are normally forbidden viewpoints.

Perspective

(Figs. 1a and 1b, page 4)
One cannot draw building and townscapes satisfactorily without studying the basics of optical law — perspective.

Eye Levels (page 4)
We start with the height from which you view your subject, that is, standing or sitting. Standing height will produce quite a different aspect to sitting. See in the illustration how other people of similar height to yourself relate to the distant building and to the horizon.

Standing height gives a high horizon in the picture with the eye level of each standing adult (similar to your own) level with the horizon. This is because the horizon line always coincides with the eye level of the artist — the most basic law of perspective. Sitting height therefore presents a lower horizon with standing figures well above the horizon level. I have projected the sight

The Ship Inn, Gabriel's Hill. 2B pencil on smooth paper.

lines of the artist through the 'picture' to the subject-matter to offer a visual check on the points made. Note how the child's height (similar to the sitting artist) coincides with the horizon.

3

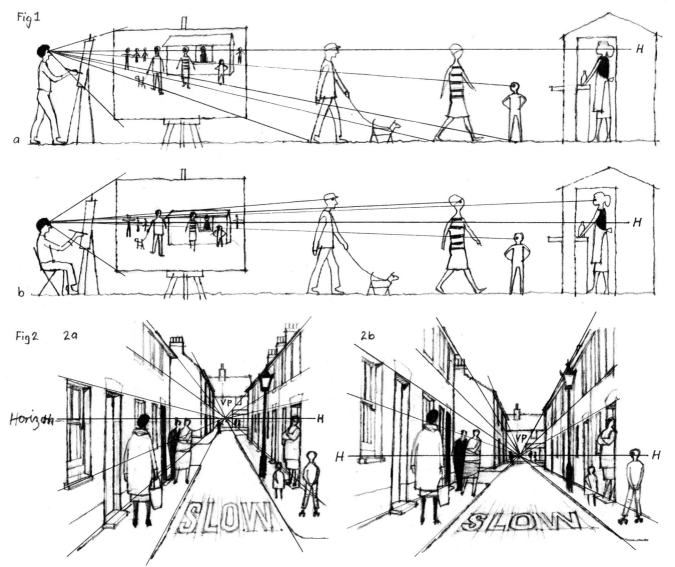

Fig 1

a

b

Fig 2   2a

Horizon

VP

H

2b

VP

H

H

SLOW

SLOW

Vanishing points

Having established our horizon or eye level we now have to determine the point on the horizon toward which parallel lines appear to converge. A good example of this can be found in any straight level road or street. The examples here show that all horizontal lines running down the length of the street — such as kerbstones, roof ridges, roof gutters, tops, bottom and horizontal glazing bars — all appear to vanish to the same point on the horizon, whether at a high or low level or if they protrude forward or lie back from the road.

This rule applies in both Figures although we have a higher horizon in the top example as seen from a standing position and then from a sitting position in the lower. Notice (Fig 2a) as in the eye level diagrams, how the eyes of the pedestrians on the pavement coincide with the horizon and your own eye level. This is not so when sitting to draw (Fig 2b) as their common eye level will appear horizontal and coincide with the horizon.

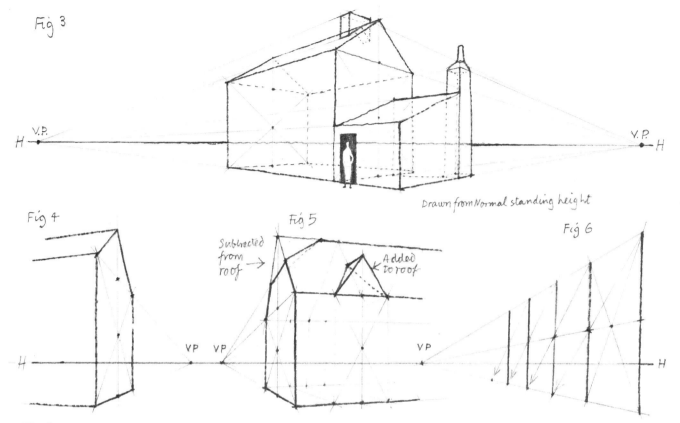

Fig 3

Drawn from Normal standing height

Fig 4

Fig 5
Subtracted from roof →
Added to roof →

Fig 6

Fig 3

Next we must consider the situation where we confront a building or group of buildings 'corner-on'. Here we will find that, although those horizontal lines still follow the same rules, converging away to the horizon, those higher than your eye level move *downwards* toward the horizon and those below eye level move *upwards* toward the horizon. This situation needs to have *two* vanishing points — both on the same horizon, each relating to the two sides of the buildings.

Fig. 4

Roofs present a challenge as their angles vary and they do not conform directly to our previous 'rules'. Find the centre line of the gable wall of the building by drawing two straight lines diagonally from corner to corner on this wall. Where they bisect each other is the centre. Draw a vertical from this point upwards to the roof ridge and complete the roof.

Fig. 5

More complicated roofs are best rendered as a basic roof with sections removed or added.

Fig. 6

Where units are of the same height and equidistant from each other: the fronts of terraced houses, lampposts, fencing posts etc., you can construct them by using an extension of the principle used in Fig. 4.

Having established the height and intervals between the first and second units, find the centre of the height on the near object and project this to the appropriate vanishing point on the horizon. This line will run through the centre of all other objects. Now draw a line diagonally from the top of the first unit downward to the point where the *centre* line runs through the second unit. Continue this line from this centre point to the line which runs through the *base* of each object and you will have found the point on which to construct the next unit.

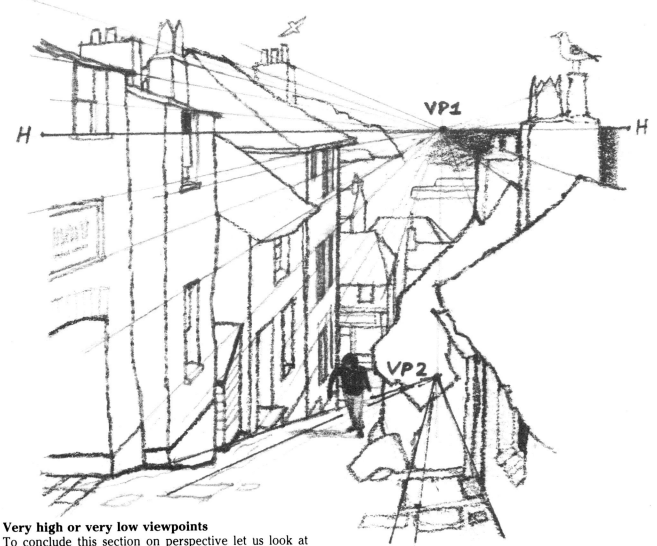

Very high or very low viewpoints

To conclude this section on perspective let us look at more extreme variations of eye levels, bearing in mind the same principle of the horizon with our rising or lowering eye level.

One of the most problematical viewpoints for the beginner is to draw a street which runs up or down a steep hill. These buildings step up on each other, therefore a shop three or four buildings on up the hill may have its base level with top of the ground floor door of the lower one. Whether we can see the distant horizon or not we have to place a 'horizon' at our eye level (H).

Fig. 7a (Downhill)

If we draw our base line for each building toward our vanishing point (on the high horizon) we shall find that we will also have to follow through with all the other lines on the same building and then so on up or down the hill from where we have chosen to start. However the sides of the street itself travel upward or downward (not parallel with the base of the building) and require their own vanishing point on their own horizon.

6

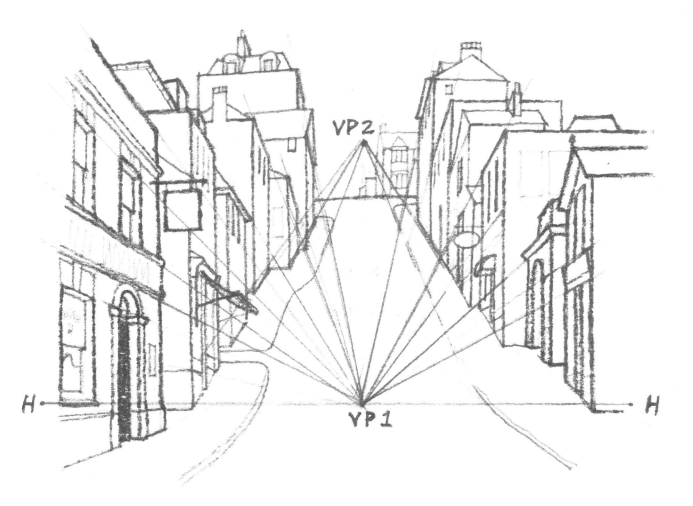

Above. *As you look uphill, the horizontal lines of the buildings converge along eye level (H) at vanishing point VP1. The street lines converge at VP2.*

Page 6. *As you look downhill, all the horizon lines of the buildings converge along eye level (H) at vanishing point VP1, while the street surface lines converge at VP2.*

Fig. 7b (Uphill)

The same principles apply to a subject where you are looking *up* a steep hill — where the horizon for the buildings will be low (level with your low eye level) and the horizon for the street itself will be much higher. In both views the 'stepping' of the buildings will appear quite strongly pronounced as the buildings are foreshortened.

A simple viewfinder or grid can be helpful provided that it is held horizontally when you are checking.

Remember, if your drawing 'looks wrong', keep checking the points discussed above and you should find with careful observation and common sense that it will come out right in the end!

Interiors

Drawing interiors — particularly your own home — can give you much valuable experience in understanding perspective and structure when studying furniture, natural still life and above all, lighting, atmosphere and mood. You can do this at leisure, in reasonable comfort and without the unwanted attentions of spectators.

When starting to draw interiors limit yourself to one or two aspects such as structure, and very simple light and shade, to emphasise the solid character of furniture, doors, windows etc. Later, try more atmospheric drawings using tone and texture — perhaps blurring the outlines here and there where the light floods in, softening the hard edges and casting interesting shadows.

In these examples you will see that in two of them I have selected smallish areas rather than a large panoramic view. I have also made use of scale changes placing comparatively small objects fairly near to my drawing position so that they can appear large in the foreground to add interest where there may well be large areas of empty floor or blank table tops. When you are working in tone, remember to check which areas are the darkest and where your source of light is placed. Usually a window showing sky or a white wall will provide the lightest tone (white paper) and you must work backwards from this toward the darkest shadows — but only very small areas are likely to be solid black.

2B pencil and carbon crayon on smooth paper.

Aboriginal craft shop, Australia. Tone is an important element when representing light. The only white paper showing here is in the window and the overhead spotlights. Sepia conté on watercolour paper.

9

Drawing from your own home

There is no home which contains nothing worth drawing outside — the windows, garden, yard or balcony can all be of interest. What to some onlookers may seem to be an 'unattractive' view of backs of other buildings or old sheds can make a most pleasant picture. Even washing on a line has its own quality. Perhaps the shapes between sheets hanging out to dry may be more rich than the sheets, as I found when looking out of a window in Cornwall. Windows' relationships to the surroundings — either reflecting sky or other windows or buildings — or open — revealing deep dark interiors, people and objects — present the artist with first-class subjects.

When drawing from a balcony or high window the problems of perspective become more evident, but do not be too anxious for absolute accuracy or your work could become too tight and hard in appearance. Try to find the characterful aspects of your subject. Very few buildings are really symmetrical and it is usually the less symmetrical aspects which offer the best material to the artist; odd angles on walls, irregular brickwork, dipping roof ridges, crooked chimneys and rich textures.

A great advantage of drawing from your home is that of choosing your weather and lighting conditions. Wet surfaces can be most rewarding to draw and reflections can enrich quite a plain and uninteresting building.

Strong shadows can also add interest and character particularly in early morning or afternoon. Twilight is a good time to work, although one has to be quick to capture the quality of that half hour or so. I would recommend you make a series of visual notes — little tonal sketches of roof silhouettes, lighted windows, street lamps, shadow etc., possibly on several separate occasions, and build them into a more 'finished' piece of work later. By this means you can capture more than would be possible in one evening, and exercise further your abilities in selectivity — reorganising your drawing by keeping only the most characterisitic elements and placing them in relation to each other to gain maximum effect with the minimum of means.

Try making several drawings of the same subject under different lighting conditions. Monet did just this in his paintings of the front of Rouen Cathedral.

Above. *Chimney stacks: HB pencil on smooth cartridge.*

Opposite. *Rooftops: pencil on tinted paper.*

Left. *Washing on the line: carbon pencil on rough watercolour paper.*

Textures

While line and tone describe the shape and general appearance of a building, you can extend the richness of your drawings by indicating with what materials it has been built. Brick, stone, iron and steel, wood, glass and concrete are the materials most commonly found. This wealth is the 'icing on the cake' when drawing buildings, for each has its own inherent surface or texture. Weather and age imperceptibly add to the patina. No wonder the artists making the Grand Tour in the eighteenth and nineteenth centuries were fascinated by ruins!

However, like icing a cake, texture should not be laid on so thick as to obliterate the main structure. While I enjoy depicting the various materials of which a building is constructed, I am careful to *indicate* rather than *portray*. I have to differentiate between what I see in front of me and what is appropriate for my drawing. In a drawing of a small detail, such as the gatepost to Conway House, it is quite feasible and appropriate to draw in all the bricks, but I would not do so when drawing a street of houses. A combination of tone and detailed

drawing is probably the best balance. Keep detail for features in the foreground or specific areas of interest.

On page 14, I show some of the ways I achieve my effects when drawing texture. Different media can be mixed with each other to provide a rich variety of visual effects that adds interest and information about the building materials.

Iron, wood, brickwork, stone, glass — these are some of the materials buildings are made of. Texture plays a vital part in making drawings of buildings interesting.

Stone buildings provide interesting surfaces, especially if the masonry is uneven.

Above. *Wooden buildings may have different textures depending on whether the structure is painted or bare.*

CONWAY HOUSE

A. Left. *Carbon pencil gives rich blacks and a marked granulated effect when used on rough paper.*

Middle. *Lead pencil provides a wide range of tones, but is softer.*

Right. *Watercolour pencil can be wetted with a brush or spit and rubbed to give continuous tone.*

B. Left. *Indent heavy watercolour paper with a dry point, then rub wax crayon over. The indentations simulate the mortar between bricks.*

Middle. *Drawn wax crayon with different pressures gives the effect of stone-built construction.*

Right. *Drawing with pen and ink outlines the separation between crumbling textures; wax crayon over gives the contrast in textures.*

C. Left. *Brush diluted Indian ink over rough watercolour paper with a stiff hog-hair brush to give a streaky texture, then draw over with a dry medium (wax crayon or carbon pencil) to render ageing woodwork.*

Right. *Draw over a diluted ink wash with pen and ink or black pencil medium to render brickwork, broken stucco, pebbledash.*

Drawing at night

Have you ever thought of drawing at night? We take daylight for granted, but night-time scenes can be strongly atmospheric — one has only to think of the illustrations to Dickens' novels, or those in children's books.

Here, detail is almost excluded, and dramatic lighting comes into its own. Shadows loom. Silhouette and mass are dominant. Arrange for there to be enough light on your sketchpad to see what you are doing but not so much as to blind you to the subject you are drawing. Good observation places are usually from windows. Try making daytime sketches, then recreate them as night scenes from memory. Pen and ink, with loose washes of diluted ink are particularly effective for portraying night scenes, as in the drawing above.

A pen and ink drawing with washes, of a wild moonlit night over country cottages. Detail is kept to a minimum — the silhouette of the chimneys and roofs is the main feature of the drawing.

When drawing this town street I was able to sit on a bench and make myself comfortable. My main interest was the facades of the shops and the public house, where the change from brick to wood cladding, stucco to stone, and the variety of the windows from one building to another provided me with a wealth of interest. I deliberately left the roofs as blank shapes for although they presented interesting changes in surface pattern, any further detail would have made my drawing look fussy. The church detail provided an interesting foil to the amorphous mass of the tree to the left. The stone trough in the left foreground gave my picture scale and depth, as did the people and cars. When composing the picture I took liberties by moving the position of the centre tree and the church tower. Otherwise I recorded what I saw.

17

Railway station. 2B pencil with carbon crayon. This view is composed entirely around a single vanishing point, situated just to the left of the telephone box. I left my perspective guidelines showing. There is an abundance of detail, but the drawing's interest lies in the dynamic of the perspective.

Industrial scenes

Many industrial subjects make excellent material for drawings. The variety of 'forms' that make them up — such as pipes, containers, structural ironwork and notices — can be seen in the same way as the roofs, windows, and facades of domestic and civil buildings.

In the examples on these pages I have contrasted the 'hard' forms — such as structural supports, parts of buildings and sign boards — with the 'soft' forms, such as shadows, smoke and water. Render the softer forms more loosely, even using a different but sympathetic medium to achieve your objective.

Our surroundings are continually being transformed into a more industrialised environment, yet this need not necessarily prevent you from finding good subject-matter. Grain or animal food silos, for example, are now a common feature on many of our more industrialised farms, and their basic circular forms often contrast excitingly with other elments in the vicinity such as machinery, vehicles and, indeed, the landscape.

Top. *I drew this oil rig from a photograph. My interest was to contrast the huge bulk of the platform with the skeletal structure of the drill. Smoke from the burn-off gave textural contrast. 4B pencil on smooth cartridge.*
Bottom. *Grain silos. The smooth cylinders provide textural contrast with the rest of my sketch. Sepia conté on sketching paper.*

Buildings in landscape

While towns and cities may have trees, flowerbeds and parks to counterpoint their essentially man-made environment, in the countryside the reverse is the case. Nowadays it would be hard to stand anywhere in the English countryside without seeing part of a village or other buildings. These visual punctuations make our drawings more interesting — there is scarcely a Constable landscape, for instance, that does not have a church or building in it as a focal point.

The study of landscape drawing is outside the scope of this book but there is a point at which the natural aspects are almost as important as the buildings that form our main subject. Historically, their fabric may be local:

Above. *In this drawing in pencil on rough watercolour paper, the blacks of the extreme shadows and windows provide a focus in what is otherwise an outline study.*

Cotswold buildings are made from that marvellous apricot-coloured stone, Welsh farmhouses are distinguished by roofs of local slate, to give but two examples. There is also the emotional aspect, where personal associations drive our creative urges to record places we have seen and liked.

When you draw buildings in landscape, try to emphasise their forms amid the trees and woods that surround them, separating them texturally so that the amorphous masses of nature will contrast with their linear rectitude.

Above. *A two-colour study in black and sepia conté crayon on rough watercolour paper. Sometimes touches of another colour add to a drawing's interest, but the second colour should always be subservient to the main drawing.*

21

Old buildings

The great bonus of studying and drawing old buildings is that, in the process, we come into contact with the historical past. Architecture is inextricably bound up with man's social and sometimes religious aspirations, and this is often reflected in the style in which our ancestors chose to build. If you have the chance, read up about the old buildings you wish to draw, for the more you know about them, the better you will understand their nature and character. Books and town guides will help: while most cathedrals and churches have on sale some kind of illustrated guide. When it comes to domestic architecture, your previous knowledge of larger buildings will help you recognise the clues as to their date and construction: details of doors and windows, the shape of roofs and chimneys, for instance, will inform you to some extent of the period to which they belong (though remember, styles linger on in small places long after they have been modified, changed or superseded in the big cities).

In the drawings on these pages and overleaf you will see how diverse my styles of drawing are, yet each, I think, expresses the character of the buildings I chose to portray. The linear style of the view over the river Arno in Florence says something about the stability of that great Renaissance city, and in the drawing of shopfronts on page 24 I have indicated, by my attention to the detail of doors and windows, that they have been converted out of late Georgian houses. The sketch of the Cornish alley looks as though it has been trodden for centuries, and the quick ballpoint pen drawing of the village church has just enough detail to be recognisable as having been mainly built in the fourteenth century, with its buttresses and Gothic decorated windows. The detail drawing of the French windows is so 'continental' in style that I added the sash window above to remind me that I saw it in England!

Florence, the river Arno. HB pencil on smooth paper.

Regency French window. HB pencil and carbon crayon on smooth cartridge.

Seaside Georgian; houses turned into shops. Notice how I have put in brickwork details and roof slates to add texture to this drawing, which is more finished than the others in this section. HB and 2B pencil on cartridge paper.

Top, right. *Harbour scene.* B pencil accented with carbon crayon on smooth cartridge.
Bottom, right. *Boatyard.* Fountain pen and black ink with smudged tones made by wetting finger and rubbing the ink.

Harbours and boatyards

Many buildings reveal their function by their shape, and this is especially true of the buildings around harbours. Great blocks of buildings indicate warehouses and this impression is reinforced by the presence about them of cranes. Conveyor belts and tall chimney stacks are clues that give away the presence of a power station (see the drawing above).

Seaports have their own fascination, for they are at the land's edge, and their commerce is the interface between land and sea transport. By contrast with land vehicles, ships have smooth curves and lines that serve as excellent linear counterpoint to the buildings. I often include part of a boat in my drawings of these sites. (Many such places have safety regulations which forbid entry to outsiders, so always check beforehand.)

Above. *Seashore from high-rise viewpoint, a hotel window. Pencil on sketching paper.*

Below. *Linear study in fine pen and black ink. The dark areas are expressed with close lines.*

Going on holiday

The features which we notice most often when we travel abroad on holiday are the buildings we see when we wander through the towns and villages.

I always take sketching material with me when I travel. A flat sketchpad takes up little room in luggage and a handful of the pens and pencils you are most used to are quite sufficient.

Sometimes I take photographs of places that interest me, but I never wholly substitute my camera for my sketchbook — rather the one complements the other. While photographs record everything, I prefer to be selective, so I augment my camera studies with sketches of detail — sometimes just line and tone studies to capture what I feel about a place. From photo and sketches I then do a finished drawing at home.

Cornish alleyway. 2B pencil on sketching paper.

Above. *Spanish windows: a quick tonal sketch in pen and wax crayon.*

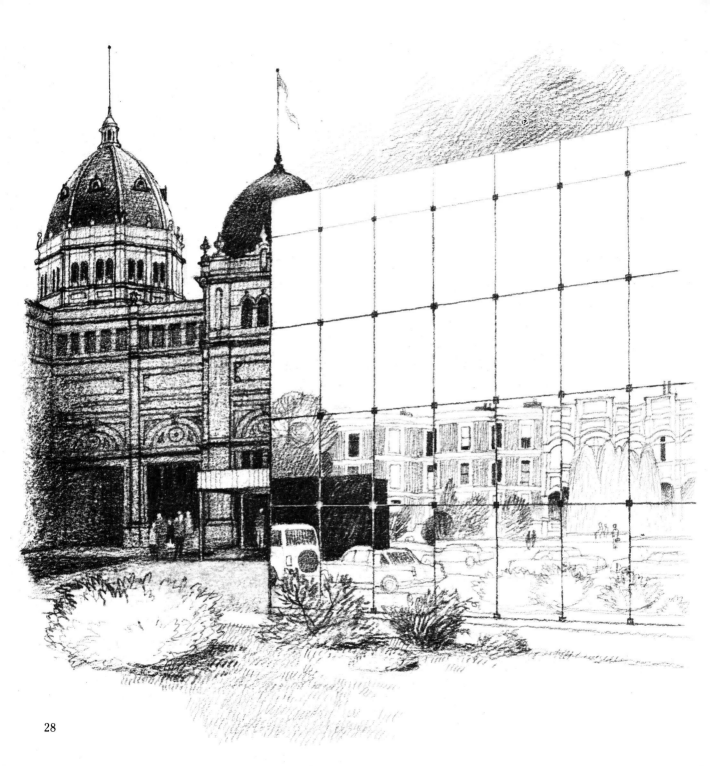

Drawing modern buildings

Most artists do not find modern buildings as attractive to draw as older, less 'tidy' architecture. However, there is an increasing number of fascinating new buildings being completed almost every day in our towns and cities, and there are many ways in which we can 'see' these buildings as new subject-matter to be explored; as, possibly, an area in which new forms of expression can flourish.

The rather uncompromising nature of much modern architecture needs other elements in the drawing to relate them to human scale and to local conditions — weather, time of day, lighting, other more established buildings, even ancient ones — and of course people, gardens, plants and traffic.

Strong perspective, even slightly exaggerated, can also add dramatic qualities but beware of over-exaggerated converging lines. They can become vulgar and destroy the character of your drawing.

One effective way to integrate modern buildings into the composition is to place them behind other, older buildings. The new ones form a backdrop to the more rich and complex architecture which has developed over a period of time.

In spite of the clean straight lines of much new architecture, refrain from using a ruler except in setting up the general masses and in checking perspective.

Large expanses of concrete or stone, even brick, can present problems. Where possible, try to vary the tone across these areas. Haze, smoke and clouds can also produce slight shadows to relieve the monotony. If they do not happen to be present when you are working 'on site', then you can produce what variation you feel to be necessary in order to balance the composition.

Above. *Melbourne office block: here I choose a view that gives architectural counterpoint to the office block. The traditional architecture in the foreground provides rich pictorial contrast to the impersonal lines of the modern building. 2B pencil and carbon crayon on cartridge paper.*

Left. *Mirror walls in modern architecture provide an interesting dimension to studies like this. Walk around such buildings to get the most dramatic reflection you can find. 2B pencil on rough watercolour paper.*

Street furniture

Besides the buildings themselves, some of the most entertaining and rewarding objects to draw in our streets and towns are items of what are called 'street furniture'. These include pillar boxes, street lamps, poster hoardings, notices and road signs, seats, tubs of plants, etc. Although the older, sometimes more ornate objects found in our streets are more popular as subjects than their clean-lined modern counterparts, the latter have good simple shapes to 'punctuate' the busy street. However, study carefully the proportions of these forms, as otherwise their authenticity in your drawing will not be convincing.

I find lettering, especially on pubs and shops, an interesting feature in depicting buildings. The drawing of the Ship Inn on page 3 shows how I incorporate this to

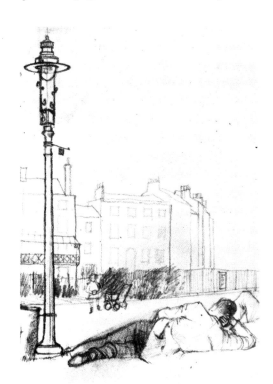

Statues, lampposts, letterboxes (the ones above were sketched when I was in Australia), road signs — all these provide subjects of interest for my sketchbook.

add visual texture and interest. Sometimes unconscious humour creeps in: the name of the sign on the drawing of the Australian shopping centre on page 32 is a comment on the old lady who is passing beneath it!

As a general rule, keep street furniture that contains strong lettering as its basic character, in the middle distance of a drawing. There it will be much easier to decide how to keep it in proportion.

Street furniture is an ideal subject for your town and building sketch books. Whenever the need arises, one can then delve into this rich source of information, and find inspiration to add to more finished work.

Shopping parade, Australia. A quick pen sketch with a humorous touch enlivens rather a dull subject.

DRAWING BUILDINGS AND TOWNS
Text and illustrations by CLIFFORD BAYLY
Series editor: Peter D. Johnson

First published 1986
by Search Press Limited
Wellwood, North Farm Road,
Tunbridge Wells, Kent TN2 3DR

Reprinted 1987 (twice), 1989

U.S. Artists Materials Trade Distributor:
Winsor & Newton, Inc.
11, Constitution Avenue, P. O. Box 1396, Piscataway, NJ 08855-1396

Canadian Distributors:
Anthes Universal Limited
341 Heart Lake Road South, Brampton, Ontario L6W 3K8

Australian Distributors:
Jasco Pty. Limited
937-941 Victoria Road, West Ryde, N.S.W. 2114

New Zealand Distributors:
Caldwell Wholesale Ltd
Wellington and Auckland

Material from this volume, text and illustrations, has previously been published in *Drawing for Pleasure* (1983), edited by Peter D. Johnson and published jointly by Search Press Ltd and Pan Books Ltd.

ISBN (UK) 0 85532 573 9
Typeset by Sprint
Printed in Spain by Elkar S. Coop, Bilbao